COMPUTERS ON THE FARM

LECTOR HOUSE PUBLIC DOMAIN WORKS

COMPUTERS ON THE FARM

DEBORAH TAKIFF SMITH

ISBN: 978-93-5614-444-6

Published: -

LECTOR HOUSE LLP
E-MAIL: lectorpublishing@gmail.com

COMPUTERS ON THE FARM

FARM USES FOR COMPUTERS, HOW TO SELECT SOFTWARE AND HARDWARE, AND ONLINE INFORMATION SOURCES IN AGRICULTURE

BY

DEBORAH TAKIFF SMITH

Cover Photo: Fran and Brian Schnarre, a farm couple from Columbia, Missouri, working at their computer. Photo by Duane Dailey, University of Missouri.

CONTENTS

COMPUTERS ON THE FARM
BY DEBORAH TAKIFF SMITH

PURPOSE OF THIS BULLETIN

How can a computer help you operate your farm better?

How do you select useful computer programs (software) and equipment (hardware)?

If you have a computer or plan to get one, what information can you obtain with your computer that will be useful for your farm operation?

This publication will help you answer such questions. It will help you evaluate and select a new system, or get more out of the one you already have.

The key components of computer systems you may want to know about are:

- Hardware—the physical equipment itself.
- Software—the computer programs on tape or disk, and
- Online sources of information—such as current market and weather information and technical reports.

This publication offers guidelines to help farmers select hardware, software, and online information. (See the glossary at the end of this publication for definitions of specialized computer terms.)

WHAT A COMPUTER CAN DO FOR YOU

You can use a microcomputer to help you—

Determine the most economical feed ration for dairy cows and other farm animals.

Schedule irrigation,

Get quick access to records,

Keep machinery inventories and depreciation schedules,

Help with tax records and making out income tax returns,

Keep livestock breeding and production records,

Keep a record of loans and cash flow to meet interest and principal payments,

Determine levels of earnings by working through a profit and loss statement and by calculating a percentage return to capital and a percentage return to equity,

Decide the optimum production choice for a particular farm in a given year, and the optimum combination of inputs to grow the crops or livestock chosen,

Store large amounts of data, and

Get current market and weather information if the microprocessor is connected via the telephone to data bases (see section on online services).

Software programs are also available in such areas as financial management, crop and field records, mailing lists for customers of certified seed and breeding stock, machinery purchase versus custom hiring, investment feasibility of building and livestock facilities, commodity price charts and tables, income taxation, marketing, soil conservation, and integrated pest management.

The computer and its associated software packages can help you do four kinds of work: (1) store and manipulate records, (2) provide analyses for management decisions, (3) control machines or monitor production, and (4) communicate faster with other people through their computers and data bases.

Recordkeeping

Many experts recommend that you start on a small scale, computerize one thing at a time, and learn as you go along—rather than trying to put information on your entire farm operation into the computer all at once. A good place to start is with farm records.

You can use microcomputers to keep track of financial records—such as cash flow, bank balances, accounts payable, accounts receivable, net worth statements, costs, and returns—as well as other records—such as livestock breeding and production reports, crop and field records, and mailing lists.

Farm Management Analysis

After computerizing the farm records, the next step would be to do simple analyses on the microprocessor. A good place to start is by analyzing data already stored in the computer or available in the files.

For example, you could use the recordkeeping capabilities of the computer to record and depreciate equipment, and to decide whether it is cheaper to lease or buy farm equipment.

General software is available to help you with accounting and bookkeeping, basic business functions.

Process Controllers

Besides analyzing farm management problems and storing data, computers have another key use—as process controllers. They can control such devices as pumps and gates, record milk output per cow, and control grain drying.

To save water and energy, some farmers have switched to sophisticated irrigation scheduling by programing their computers to read the moisture in the soil, the weather, and the humidity, and to provide information on a plant's age and irrigation needs. The computer then tells the farmer when to water a crop and for how long—and can even turn the water on and off.

Telecommunications

You can also use a computer as an up-to-date source for communication, linking you to banks of information that are available almost instantaneously from public and private online information sources. With the computer hooked up to the telephone, you can get information quickly, receive it visually, and record it in detail if you wish.

Some key information sources are listed on page 20 of this bulletin.

Other Uses

Farm families can use microcomputers the same way other families do—to plan the family budget, keep an inventory of household furnishings, keep track of recipes, keep mailing lists, turn lights and heat on and off, type homework and other documents, learn new skills, and play games.

COMPUTERS ON THE FARM

Most of the computers farmers are getting are microcomputers, also called home computers or personal computers. They are the basis of the "computer revolution" that has been occurring since the late 1970's and they are the focus of this publication.

Many farmers, especially the owners of the larger farms, already have computers. But you don't have to be a large farmer to afford a microcomputer. Computers can be useful in almost all areas of a farming operation—helping you decide what, when, and how to plant; how to sell; and how to arrange the farm business to be more efficient and more profitable.

The computer can supplement the calculator, typewriter, and file cabinet. And it can send and receive written or graphic messages by telephone (in most areas of the country) that might be too long or complex to do verbally.

A computer can be very useful when repetitive analyses are needed or when data storage is important, as with financial records or daily milk output per cow.

More and more, farming requires sophisticated management decisions and management of basic resources, including land, water, labor, production inputs, and capital. These are the kinds of decisions the computer can help you make faster and more cost-effectively.

Although a computer program for your farm operation could make record-keeping and analysis easier and improve your ability to manage, it might be hard to measure these improvements in dollars. But the dollars you save by having better information on when to sell a crop, how to monitor the business, and how to diagnose a problem before it gets out of control might pay for the computer. Farmers and ranchers with large feedlot or other livestock operations might find that a feed formulation program could cut costs enough to pay for the computer system within a few months.

HOW TO CHOOSE A MICROCOMPUTER SYSTEM

Should you buy a microcomputer? How do you decide on a system that's best for you? Here are some factors to consider in making these decisions.

The first step is to think about your needs. What would you do with your computer system? How would you actually use it to help you run your operation better? List your primary needs, the important things you want to do right away with your computer. Then, think of secondary needs—things you might do in the future once you have a computer.

Once you've identified your needs, the next step is to shop around—to find some software that fulfills your needs and to see some systems in operation. Go to computer stores or get in touch with the salespeople in your area. You could decide to have custom programs written for your operation, but they will be significantly more expensive than programs that have already been developed.

Talk to other farmers, ranchers, extension and university specialists, and business people who are using microcomputers. Find out what software they are using. Do some research (by reading books or magazines, taking a course or seminar, or visiting a trade show) so you'll be an informed customer when you shop seriously.

Many computer experts strongly recommend against buying a computer first and then shopping for the software packages. So identify your needs and select the software packages or materials that will help you do what you want to with your computer. Then find the hardware to run the programs.

The Computer Revolution

"The advent of computers to farm management ... is already underway and seems likely to have a powerful influence," said USDA historian Wayne Rasmussen in 1982. "The computer should lead to more efficient management of machines and energy and should help in other farming operations such as cost accounting, mixing feed rations and applying fertilizers and other resources efficiently. Some farmers now have computers of their own, and many others have access to computer systems through their county agricultural agents," Rasmussen pointed out.

The computer can be seen as the "third revolution" in American farming. The first revolution was the use of the horse, which added animal power to human power. The second was the switch from the horse to the tractor, which again expanded the power an individual could wield. But the computer is a different kind of technological advance because it adds to the farmer's power to manage.

By 1990, the computer will probably be as important a part of a commercial farmer's operation as the pickup truck. Farmers may flip on their computers first thing in the morning—instead of their radios—to get the latest market prices. They can get a rundown on weather and growing conditions for major worldwide production areas; pertinent data on prices, market conditions, credit terms, transportation and storage rates, and related forecasts; and finally a list of priorities each day to take advantage of these conditions.

Getting the right system—the combination of hardware (the physical equipment) and software (the computer programs)—is the problem farmers must solve before they can make the most of the computer revolution.

STRATEGIES FOR GETTING INTO COMPUTERS

If you're interested in getting your farm's operations computerized, and you're just starting, you could choose various strategies for doing so. One way is to first buy the basic hardware and components you think you need, and then add memory and other components later. If you do that, be sure you can add additional disk drives, memory, and a printer to your computer, all at a reasonable cost.

What can you do with a small computer once you outgrow it, and you want to get a bigger one? You might want to use your older computer in a small, specialized farm operation, or keep it to retrieve and analyze records that you stored on the old equipment. Other alternatives would be to trade it in on a larger computer, advertise to sell it through the local want-ads, trade or sell it to a friend or neighbor, keep the small computer for someone else in the family (perhaps a game-playing youngster), or donate it to a local school or religious or charitable group and take a tax write-off.

The farm of the future may have many computers, some for specific functions such as irrigation scheduling or dairy operations, and one for financial records. Having several computers would help farmers deal with the problem of malfunctioning computers, so that the whole farm would not be shut down if one computer goes down.

ALTERNATIVES TO BUYING A MICROCOMPUTER

You might consider alternatives to buying a computer. You may be able to lease one to see what it will do for you, and use it until your needs make it worthwhile to buy one. Prices keep coming down. The best time to buy is when you find you can profitably make use of a computer. Even though it becomes technically obsolete, it will still do for you what you purchased it for.

A programmable calculator may be an appropriate tool that is much less costly then a microcomputer.

If you like what a computer can do for your operation but aren't ready to buy one or to use it yourself, you might hire a consultant to help you select an appropriate system. Or you might retain an accountant or computer consultant to run the financial analysis programs you need. This kind of service gives quick results, and relieves you of having to do it yourself.

INFORMATION AVAILABLE FROM
YOUR COUNTY EXTENSION AGENT

State Cooperative Extension Services are helping States provide computers for county offices. Many State Extension Services already have computers in nearly every county Extension office.

If you are considering buying or leasing a computer system, or want software or timesharing services to make the most of the system you have, a good place to go is to your State or county Extension office. In many States, county Extension offices have terminals connecting them to mainframe computers; some have microcomputers which give them access to information on crop management, animal production, and marketing.

The county Extension staff can tell you what is available online in your area that is tailored to your kind of farming and your region. The Extension staff will also be able to tell you the software programs applicable in your State. Many State Extension offices have publications on computers, and others have or are developing online information networks linking farmers and other users to the State university mainframe computer and its data base.

State Extension specialists are a logical place to start when looking for software that is appropriate to your needs. Many State Extension computer and agricultural experts have produced software materials that are available, and the county agent will know about them.

In some cases the county Extension office can lend you software. If you don't have a computer, the Extension office may be able to run programs for you, choosing the appropriate software available and plugging in the precise conditions and problems on your farming or ranching operation. Or they may be able to use the computer to search for information you need, perhaps communicating with a large State, regional, or national data base.

As lower cost computers with improved software have become available, an increasing number of people are turning to their State Cooperative Extension Services for training in computer fundamentals, equipment selection, and software evaluation. County agents can help people find what is available, but they probably will not be preparing software programs themselves.

HOW TO SELECT SOFTWARE

The key criteria for selecting good software are the following: Does it meet your needs? Does it do what it says it will do? And does it have good support documentation?

Checklist for Evaluating Software

Here are some factors to consider when evaluating and comparing software:

Documentation. Look at the "documentation" or the written (paper) materials that come with your program. These should explain clearly what the program does and what you have to do to use it.

Ease of Use. Is the program fairly easy to use? Does it guide you through the program?

Instructions. Another factor you should consider in evaluating software is the instructions. Are there instructions in the program or in the written documentation? Are they readable? You should be sure you understand how to operate the program.

Help. What help can you get if you run into problems? Does the program have a "help" function? When you don't know how to answer a question or need help, can you turn to a separate part of the computer program or to a part of the accompanying documentation to answer your question? Is there a company phone-in service you can call if you need help?

Some software programs may come to you with bugs (errors) in them. Find out what backup services are available. Is there a hotline you can call for help if the program has a problem you can't solve? Does the company provide updated versions periodically? Are they free or at nominal cost?

Compatibility with Hardware. Is the software compatible with hardware you already have, or does it run on an operating system you can use with your hardware?

Some computers use tape cassettes, like audio tape you use on a tape recorder. The most standard storage medium for programs and data is the floppy diskette, which looks like a soft phonograph record. The diskette comes in several sizes— the most common are 8 inches and 5¼ inches. A newer possibility is the 8-inch hard disk. The hard disk may be used for storage, but you buy the software on a floppy disk and transfer it.

Memory. Does your computer have enough memory to run the program?

Recommendation. Does the program come from a reputable source, or does it come with a recommendation from someone you trust?

Effectiveness. Does the program do what you want it to do correctly and consistently?

Where to Look for Good Software

Where do you find good software? Some farmers and ranchers write their own programs or pay a programmer to write a custom program. But most get existing programs either from State Extension sources or from commercial outlets.

Many operations farmers need to perform on a computer can be done by using generalized software packages readily available through commercial sources.

Check with your County Extension Agent. He or she may know of the programs that have been tailored for your operation. The Extension Service has published a directory of agricultural software programs produced by State Extension Services, entitled "Updated Inventory of Agricultural Computer Programs."[1]

[1] To order a copy, send $3.50, payable to the University of Florida, to

There are also various private directories of software that is compatible for particular equipment. You can get these programs at computer stores or through mail-order sources. Many trade journals carry ads of agricultural software vendors.

The land-grant university in your State may have computer programs available for farmers at nominal cost. Many States have produced extensive computer software. There are also many commercial software houses that produce computer programs in the field of agriculture. The best programs are written by people who combine strong expertise in the agricultural subject matter with the ability to write good computer programs that are relatively "friendly" or easy to use.

The 1980's have seen a big jump in the number, quality, and friendliness of agricultural software. But you still need to evaluate carefully the programs you are considering. Remember that software selection and evaluation are important factors to consider when planning a computer system for your farm.

COMPATIBILITY COUNTS

Computers and marriages should share one thing in common: Compatibility. If it's not there, the system won't work.

Not all hardware and software are compatible. In fact, hundreds of producers of computer equipment and computer programs are in the market, and there are few across-the-board standards. So it's important to get hardware and software that are compatible.

Software, or the computer programs themselves, are not like records that can be played on any record player. They have to be compatible with the hardware in terms of the programing language used, operating system, size, format, and other factors.

Try to find a store in your area where you will get the expertise you need to obtain the right combination of software and hardware to meet your needs.

When you buy a computer, find out whether it comes with a standard operating language that will allow you to use a wide variety of programs written in different languages on your computer. Even then, you may find that a disk that supposedly works with that operating language will not work on your machine.

HOW TO SELECT HARDWARE

Checklist for Evaluating Hardware

Here are some factors to consider when evaluating and comparing hardware:

Software. The first questions to ask are, "What software do you plan to use?" and "Which computer will run that program?"

Administrative Services
Institute of Food and Agricultural Sciences (IFAS) Bldg. 664
University of Florida
Gainesville, FL.

Does the computer come with a standard operating system so that it will be compatible with a range of software programs?

Memory. How much memory, or information storage capacity, do you need? The computer's memory is measured in kilobytes (abbreviated K), and most computers come in sizes ranging from 2K up to 256K. (A kilobyte is equal to roughly 1,000 characters.) You need to know the software program you will use and your recordkeeping requirements to accurately estimate the capacity of the equipment you need.

Some agricultural programs use 48K or 64K of memory. User friendly programs, which require little training to use and which guide you through the program, may be easier; but they may require more memory for the program itself, leaving you less storage space or memory for the data.

Computation. What kind of computational ability do you want your computer to have? Will it serve the computing needs you have identified for now and later?

Input and Output Devices. What kind of output do you need? What additional pieces of equipment or peripherals (such as separate screen, disk drive, modem, printer) will you need to buy to make this system do what you want it to?

Most agricultural programs require a printer. A dot matrix printer (which produces characters made of small dots) may be sufficient. Another option is a letter quality printer, which is more expensive.

How big a screen do you need? (Screens are measured in characters and in inches.) Do you need an 80-column or 40-column monitor? Do you need color and strong graphics capability? What quality screen image do you need?

Can you add memory and other components later if you need to?

External Storage. What kind of external storage does the system use, floppy disk, hard disk, or tape? Cassette tape storage costs less, but compared to disk storage, it has several disadvantages.

If the hardware uses floppy disks, is the disk drive included as part of the computer package or does it come separately? Is a second disk drive included in the package or does it come separately? What kind of a disk drive(s) do you need, single or double density? Hard or floppy?

Training. What training is available in the use of the new equipment?

Backup and Maintenance Services. What backup and maintenance services are available from the vendor or other sources, once you've bought this computer?

What happens when the computer is down (not working)? Does the company or store from which you plan to buy offer a service contract, and how much does it cost? Will you have to carry your computer to their site for servicing, and how long are you likely to be without it? How far away is your dealer and where will the computer actually be serviced?

It's important to buy something that you can have fixed fairly quickly and cheaply, since elements of your system, especially the mechanical parts, may well need repair at some time.

Value. What equipment and software programs come with the basic package, and are these items included in the base price?

Compare prices carefully, considering the components and software you are getting for a particular price. Do not buy on the basis of price alone, but consider also the reliability of the equipment and the vendor, and the service you will be getting to set up, maintain, and support your system.

Where to Look for Good Hardware

Many buyers get their computers at specialty stores that handle computers and other electronics. Some handle only one brand of computer. It's worthwhile to shop around and see various systems. The big national department store chains sell computers, too. Talk to your neighbors about what they're using, and be sure to get hands-on practice with systems you are considering.

Try to find a reputable dealer who can offer backup support. Consider the pros and cons of getting all equipment from a single vendor versus shopping around for peripherals from different manufacturers. A reliable dealer who handles several brands can help you make this decision.

Check with your Extension office. It may have a State publication on computers or a checklist for buying one.

Types of Hardware

Farmers are using several different types of computers. Besides the microcomputer, which is the most widely used, other kinds of farm computers include interactive terminals, videotex terminals, handheld processors, and minicomputers.

A microcomputer can be used as a stand-alone unit, working on its own with a software disk or tape. Or it can be connected to outside information sources if it is equipped with a device known as a modem, which allows the computer to communicate with other computers over the telephone. The modem turns the computer from an information processor and storage machine into a piece of communications equipment.

An interactive terminal has no data storage capability but is linked to a central computer through the telephone. This is called a "dumb" terminal because it can receive, display, and send information, but it cannot process that information. Programs and data are stored in the central computer and the user pays a fee to access the system.

A videotex keyboard terminal can be connected to a telephone jack and any television set. The user can request and receive any kind of information stored in the central computer. Some of the online services use this type of equipment (see section about online information systems on page 20).

Many farmers are also using handheld programmable calculators. These are convenient to use in the field, and can record often repeated data, such as daily milk production. They have little memory (usually 2K) and their output can be printed on 2-inch paper tape. They are much cheaper than the microcomputer.

Farmers use them to record daily milk production, formulate dairy and beef rations, estimate value of dairy forages, estimate cost of operating farm machinery, and calculate depreciation and investment tax credit.

Some very large farm operations use minicomputers, which are larger, have more memory, can do more functions than the microcomputers, and can support multiple users. However, the newer microcomputers have more memory and more functions, and the difference between minicomputers and microcomputers has narrowed.

Computer System Components

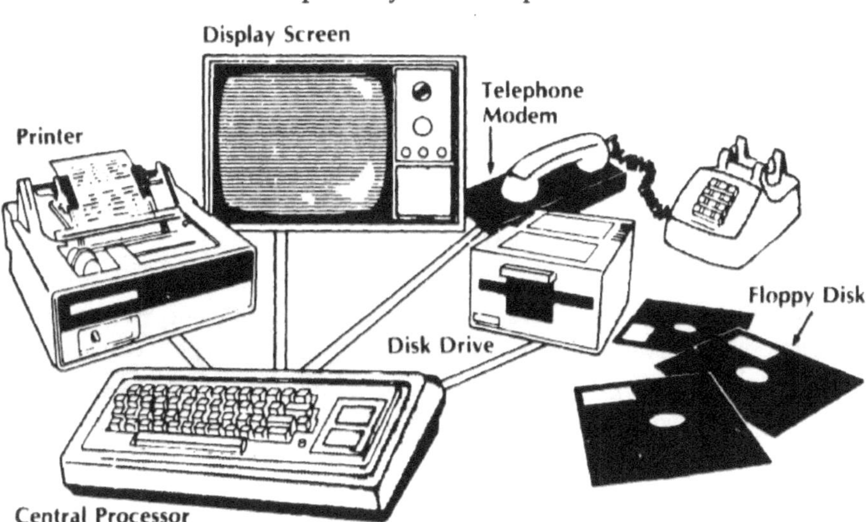

COMPONENTS OF A MICROCOMPUTER

One way to understand how a microcomputer works is to see its key components.

The **central processing unit** (CPU) is the silicon chip that is the "brain" of the computer. It does all the computation and controls all the other processing.

The CPU stores **memory** of several kinds. Part of the memory is wired into the computer permanently by the manufacturer. This is called Read Only Memory (ROM). It contains such things as the operating system and program language. Random Access Memory (RAM) is the memory bank that includes the computer program or instructions, as well as the data. Your storage devices—tape cassettes, floppy disks, or hard disks—that store computer programs and data, are sometimes called external memory.

The computer system also needs **input devices** and **output devices**. Your keyboard is an input device; disk drives and tape drives are also input devices. The output will probably be a cathode ray tube (CRT), which looks like a video monitor. The printer is the other output device you may choose to include in your computer system.

Make sure the microcomputer has an adequate number of input and output ports for future needs.

If you use your computer for communications, you'll need a telephone **modem**.

Here is a possible shopping list of hardware for a farmer's starting microcomputer system:

CPU (computer) with 48K or 64K of memory.

CRT or monitor with adequate character width for the programs you plan to use.

One or two disk drives, either 5¼ or 8 inches in diameter.

Dot matrix printer (optional).

Modem for communication with large computer (optional).

TRY IT OUT

Be sure you try the system you plan to buy. Test run on a sample problem the hardware and software combination you are considering using. See if you think the solutions the computer puts out are what you need.

If you insist on a thorough demonstration of the material you are considering buying, you can evaluate it in terms of its ease of use and the usefulness of its analysis.

If you're thinking of buying a new software package for a computer you already have, ask to try it out first. Some software distributors in the public sector will give you a trial period to make sure the program is satisfactory and runs on your equipment. Or you may be able to obtain a demonstration disk. At least, try out new programs with the same microprocessor, printer, and screen you use to make sure they will work on your equipment.

It's useful to have software evaluated by a reputable source—for example your local county Extension agent, State Extension specialist, or a neighbor who has had experience.

"Let the buyer beware" is a good motto to remember as you shop around for a computer system.

Getting Comfortable with Computers

If you can use a typewriter, you can use a computer. Most agricultural program's do not require particular math or technical skills, just a knowledge of your farming operation and the ability to think in a logical, orderly way. Most new programs are user friendly; they ask you questions in plain English, and you type the answer on the keyboard.

A good way to feel comfortable with computers is to try one out at your local computer store, or at fairs, conferences, or workshops at universities.

COMPUTERS NEED AN INVESTMENT IN TIME AND MONEY

In addition to considering the cost of a computer system, consider the time and effort it takes to learn the equipment and the programs, and to keep records. Who will be operating the microcomputer? Does he or she have the patience and skills to learn to operate the computer, and to enter the large amounts of data that will be required initially?

The computer may save time and money. Many farmers find that they don't save time but they accomplish more in the time they do spend. Don't underestimate the amount of time and effort it will require to collect data, make sure it's accurate, enter the data, and run the analyses.

It's important to consider how user-friendly the computer is, and how much the computer's software will do to guide you through the analysis.

A computer will do calculations very quickly, perhaps saving hours of laborious figuring. A computer will store information from one time period to the next, and recalculate alternatives quickly. By making the information available, it will help you identify strong and weak points in your operation.

However, these functions will depend on your data. If the records you use in making a computation are incomplete, for example, the computer cannot fill in the gaps for you nor overcome inaccuracies in the data.

INFORMATION AVAILABLE ONLINE FROM USDA, STATE, AND PRIVATE SOURCES

You can transform your own microprocessor or other computer into a powerful communications device by adding a modem to it and communicating over the telephone.

This will help you gather information on news, weather forecasts, emergencies or disasters, crop and livestock production, and marketing (including current and future prices).

Online computer services also include buying and selling farm products; purchasing farm and home supplies, including teleshopping; banking services; business management advice; ordering theater tickets; information concerning farm and public policy; and personal education and entertainment.

Many farmers who are computerizing their operations, as well as others in agriculture, can use some form of online information. There are more than 1,300 public and private information sources available on computer. New ones seem to come out every week. The following selected list of information you can receive on computer includes some of the major private online information services with agricultural applications, as well as the main ones available from USDA and the State land-grant institutions.

Most of these information networks are paid for by the user based on the amount of use. Many charge an initial fee, and then most charge the user by the amount of time he or she spends on the system.

No one computer system or online system may be adequate for everyone. There are many good systems, and different systems are good for different tasks.

1. AGNET

AGNET is a major online information and problem-solving service for farmers, ranchers, agribusinesses, and homes. It is sponsored jointly by five State Cooperative Extension Services—Nebraska, Montana, North Dakota, South Dakota, and Washington—and operated by the University of Nebraska. County Extension offices in several States participate, and farmers in nearly all the 50 States and Canada subscribe to AGNET.

It helps people make marketing and production decisions and solve agricultural management problems, and it provides current information on market conditions and news items. It offers cash and futures market reports, international market reports from the U.S. Department of Agriculture (USDA) Foreign Agricultural Service (FAS), reports and report abstracts from the USDA's Economic Research Service and Statistical Reporting Service, and market comments by Extension Service economists. Also available are electronic mail service and electronic conferencing, which allows groups of users with similar interests to share ideas and information.

Farmers and ranchers who have computer terminals with communication capability can access AGNET. Others can tap into AGNET through their county Extension services. AGNET subscribers are typically agricultural lenders and bankers. Extension specialists, farm managers, home economists, agricultural consulting firms, farmers and ranchers, and exporters of agricultural commodities.

ADDRESS: AGNET
          University of Nebraska
          105 Miller Hall
          University of Nebraska
          Lincoln, NE 68583

2. AGRICOIA

AGRICOIA is an online information service produced by the National Agricultural Library (NAD of USDA), and is available commercially from a number of sources (including DIALOG and Bibliographic Retrieval Services). It provides comprehensive access to information on published literature pertaining to agriculture.

AGRICOIA is the catalog and index for NAL and covers materials published since 1970. It includes about 1.5 million citations.

AGRICOIA contains citations to worldwide published books, serial titles, and journal articles on agriculture and related subjects. In addition to bibliographic citations of published literature, the system offers information through several specialized subfiles; these subfiles include brucellosis (BRU), environmental impact statements covering 1977 and 1978 (ENV), and the Food and Nutrition Information Center, which emphasizes human nutrition research and education and food technology (FNC).

Librarians are the main users of this system.

ADDRESS: To find out more about AGRICOIA, contact:
          Educational Resources Staff
          National Agricultural Library
          Room 1402
          Beltsville, MD 20705

3. AgriData Network

AgriData is a private information and computing network specializing in agriculture. It offers immediate access to more than 10,000 pages of continuously updated business, financial, marketing, weather, and price information, as well as analyses and recommendations from its own and other reporters, analysts, economists, meteorologists, and researchers.

It offers several different services, including an online computing service that allows users to access a library of microcomputer software programs that can be transferred to the user's microcomputer; an agricultural production technology service offering data bases from 40 land-grant universities and from agricultural, chemical, fertilizer, equipment, seed, and feed companies; an "electronic yellow pages," or product service directory for farmers; and electronic mail.

ADDRESS: AgriData Resources, Inc.
          205 West Highland Ave.
          Milwaukee, WI 53203

4. Agri-Markets Data Service (AMDS)

Agri-Markets Data Service is an agricultural data base service offered by Capital Publications in Arlington, Va.

The service provides market information, such as prices and shipments, as well as commentary and other information. It gives daily and weekly market commentary on local and national market activity in livestock, grain, fruits and vegetables, and poultry and dairy products.

ADDRESS: Agri-Markets Data Service
          1300 North 17th St., Suite 1600
          Arlington, VA 22209

5. AMS Market News Network

The USDA Agricultural Marketing Service (AMS) has a Market News Tele-communications System that reports up-to-the-minute information on commodity prices, demand, and movement. The system transmits between 700 and 900 different reports each day on more than 150 farm commodities. Each report is re-transmitted an average of 30 times. The initial use of this market news system is to transmit reports to the news media and among market news offices; firms and individuals may also subscribe at their own cost.

In addition, AMS and the Public Broadcasting Service deliver market information directly to farmers via a television captioning system called Farm Market INFODATA, available in several cities around the country. By selecting a special channel on a closed captioning decoder, anyone within the broadcast coverage area of the participating public television station may receive the market information. Additional stations in a number of States have instituted this service on their own.

> For more information, contact:
> AMS Communications and Operations Branch
> Administrative Services Division, Room 0092
> U.S. Department of Agriculture
> Washington, D.C. 20250

6. AutEx Systems

AutEx Systems designs and operates computer-based communications systems which link buyers and sellers in specific industries. Two agricultural services are its Produce Network and its Floral Marketing Network.

Subscribers to the networks use AutEx supplied terminals to access a nationwide communications network that includes buyer and seller offers. This online data communications system offers pretrading information. The terminal prints information needed to compare buying and selling opportunities in fresh fruits and vegetables, as well as floral products. The company is owned by Xerox.

> ADDRESS: AutEx Systems
> 55 William St.
> Wellesley, MA 02181

7. Chase Econometrics

Chase Econometrics, a subsidiary of Chase Manhattan Bank, offers economic and financial information and analyses in the areas of industrial economics, energy, fertilizer, minerals, debenational economics, U.S. economics, and agriculture through its information system. Data and forecasting services on agribusiness cover international, national, regional, and statewide levels. Subscribers receive regular reports and analyses, and also have access to a number of historical and forecast data bases acquired through internal data collection activities or from other organizations. Many of its customers are large food and agribusiness firms.

ADDRESS: Chase Econometrics
          150 Monument Rd.
          Bala Cynwyd, PA 19004

8. CMN (Computerized Management Network)

Developed by Virginia Polytechnic Institute and State University as a national information system for use by State Extension Services, CMN helps Extension workers in solving problems, retrieving information, and evaluating programs. To date, many CMN programs have provided the foundation for several highly successful Extension programs. Two of the most popular are the Simplified Dairy Cattle Feeding Program, which has had a substantial impact on the economics of feeding dairy herds, and COIN, which provides low-cost user access to USDA reports on marketing, futures, and summary information on all major crops and livestock enterprises. The CMN system is designed to be used by people who have no special training with computers, and is available nationwide and in Canada.

ADDRESS: CMN
          Virginia Cooperative Extension Service
          Plaza I, Bldg. D
          Blacksburg, VA 24061

9. COIN (Computerized Outlook and Information Network)

COIN is a nationwide source of information from the Extension Service, which can be accessed by State and county extension staff, as well as by researchers, farmers, and agribusiness. It contains USDA outlook, market, and other information on a national computer network.

Information from the USDA which is available through COIN includes Statistical Reporting Service (SRS) Crop Reporting Board reports. Economic Research Service (ERS) economic situation summaries. World Agricultural Outlook Board reports on world agriculture supply and demand. Foreign Agricultural Service (FAS) weekly roundup of world production and trade reports. Agricultural Marketing Service (AMS) summary of daily grain market prices, and USDA news releases.

Some States use a multi-State computer network, or an in-State computer system, or both, to transfer agricultural outlook and production information to county offices and disseminate it to the general public. State Extension outlook specialists load their outlook analyses directly onto COIN (with a remote terminal) many times throughout the year.

COIN is available on the Computerized Management Network (CMN) and through USDA ONLINE (see those entries on this list).

10. CompuServe

CompuServe Information Service offers access to more than 500 data bases. Some of the subjects of particular interest to farmers include agribusiness, agricultural news, finance and investment, news, weather, specific commodities including cotton futures prices and cattle prices, and the Commodity News Service data. It also offers electronic shopping and banking, electronic mail, hobby and special interest newsletters, and games.

ADDRESS: CompuServe Incorporated
5000 Arlington Centre Blvd.
Post Office Box 20212
Columbus, OH 43220

11. CRIS—Current Research Information System

CRIS—Current Research Information System—is a computer based information storage and retrieval system. It covers most of the Nation's publicly supported agricultural and forestry research, and contains about 30,000 summaries of research projects. The data base is updated monthly. CRIS summaries provide information about ongoing research projects conducted or sponsored by USDA research agencies, 58 State agricultural experiment stations, 17 State forestry schools, 28 schools of veterinary medicine, 16 land-grant colleges of 1890, Tuskegee Institute, and other cooperating State institutions. It went online in 1977.

Through this retrieval system, an individual can obtain a brief description of the research, along with the investigators' names, performing organization and location, current progress, and a list of the latest publications resulting from the research.

CRIS inhouse search services are provided primarily to research scientists and research managers in USDA and State participating institutions. The public can directly access the CRIS data base through the DIALOG online retrieval system.

Researchers in public and private institutions are the main users of CRIS.

ADDRESS: Customer Service
DIALOG Information Retrieval Services, Inc.
3460 Hillview Avenue
Palo Alto, CA 94340

12. DRI (Data Resources, Inc.)

DRI is a private forecasting service with regional models that forecast acreage planted and harvested, and yield for all commodities. This service does independent forecasts of production, prices, and demand for livestock, and has a separate program for fertilizer. DRI has software programs for potato producers. Some of its main clients are big agricultural supply companies and food processing firms.

ADDRESS: Data Resources, Inc.
24 Hartwell Ave.
Lexington, MA 02173

13. ESTEL (Extension Service Telecommunication System)

ESTEL is a pilot project from the University of Maryland's Cooperative Extension Service. It provides farmers with information via a microprocessor or videotex equipment, which receives the information and displays it on a video screen. The videotex equipment may be cheaper to purchase than a microcomputer.

ESTEL provides current information on market news, local weather conditions, pesticides, production information, and energy conservation tips, as well as home economics and 4-H programs.

ADDRESS: ESTEL (Extension Sevice Telecommunication System)
Maryland Cooperative Extension Service
University of Maryland
College Park, MD 20742

14. Farm Bureau ACRES

The American Farm Bureau Federation has a program to provide marketing information and advice for its members. Known as Farm Bureau ACRES, this marketing information project involves several State farm bureaus. AFBF members can retrieve information from the host computers via telephone hookup and, at the same time, send messages to State computers, thereby providing a two-way daily contact between State coordinators and farmer-members. For more information, contact your county or State Farm Bureau.

15. Firsthand

Based on French videotex technology known as "Teletel," Firsthand is a transactional videotex system originally started by the First Bank System of Minneapolis and now available in other areas too. With this system, participants can access agribusiness bookkeeping systems; weather, commodity, and financial reports; and domestic and international news through a local telephone number. Clients can also do their shopping electronically from a catalog, and obtain commodity reports and other agribusiness information offered by other information providers. They can see their bank statements and balances, make transfers between accounts, and pay bills electronically.

ADDRESS: Videotex
220 Soo Line Bldg.
Minneapolis, MN 55402

16. Grassroots

Grassroots is a Canadian videotex system that provides agribusiness with comprehensive, up-to-date information. It helps farmers make effective purchasing, operating, financing, and marketing decisions. It offers market information on current and future prices of all major agricultural commodities, and carries farm management programs as well. It also offers information from companies offering products and services of interest to agriculture, including material on chemicals, fertilizers, equipment, real estate, seed, feed, grain, and livestock. Material on financial services, banking, and insurance is updated daily.

ADDRESS: Infomart
164 Merton St.

Toronto, Ontario, CANADA M4S 3A8

17. Instant Update

Instant Update is a timesharing information delivery system designed for the Professional Farmers of America. The system offers its users a variety of services and information, including electronic mail, agribusiness news and analyses, weather reports, and technical information.

ADDRESS: Instant Update
Professional Farmers of America
219 Parkade
Cedar Falls, IA 50613

18. Market Data Systems, Inc.

Market Data Systems carries information from 13 commodity exchanges for the benefit of customers. It leases terminals on which to receive the information.

ADDRESS: Market Data Systems, Inc.
3835 lamar Ave.
Memphis, TN 38118

19. NEMA (National Electronic Marketing Association, Inc.)

NEMA offers marketing firms computerized marketing systems for many agricultural products. It is a way of linking buyers and sellers without having to first transport the products to market.

Electronic marketing enables buyers and sellers to negotiate transactions in a public market while remaining in their own offices. NEMA is developing several marketing systems for agricultural markets. NEMA was developed by Virginia Tech Extension and Research staff in cooperation with the Virginia Department of Agriculture and Commerce and AMS.

Through a telephone hookup to computer terminals in any location, buyers and sellers are brought together at a specific time to determine the price, on a competitive basis, for the products being offered for sale. Prospective buyers can obtain written descriptions of the products before sale time.

One pricing technique is a computerized auction process, where the computer acts as the auctioneer. During the auction, the computer drops the asking price until a bid is received, then raises the price from that point until there is only one bidder left. At the end of a sale, the highest bidders receive summaries of their purchases. The products are shipped efficiently from seller to buyer.

State Cooperative Extension Services, producers' organizations. State departments of agriculture, and other agencies have developed and implemented NEMA, as well as some other electronic marketing systems in the United States. Today computerized systems sell slaughter and feeder livestock, cotton, and shell eggs.

This system is for market agents and buyers.

ADDRESS: National Electronic Marketing Assn., Inc.
          P.O. Box 722
          Christiansburg, VA 24073

20. NPIRS (National Pesticide Information Retrieval System)

NPIRS is a nationally accessible online data base containing information about all pesticides registered with the Environmental Protection Agency, and indicating which are registered for use against specific pests on specific crops or sites. States can also insert information about State pesticide registrations. Purdue University is developing the system under a cooperative agreement with USDA and is managing the data base, which uses facilities provided by Martin-Marietta, Inc.

ADDRESS: National Pesticide Information Retrieval System
          Entomology Hall
          Purdue University
          West Lafayette, IN 47907

21. Rural Ventures

Rural Ventures offers courses and data, recommends solutions to problems of small farmers, and promotes economic efficiency in small-scale agriculture and food processing enterprises. It is a joint venture by Control Data Corporation and other groups, which started with a project in Princeton, Minnesota.

A Rural Venture project gives farmers the capability to determine the optimum selection of crops, livestock, and equipment, and offers a full range of computer-based education and training programs.

ADDRESS: Rural Ventures, Inc.
          120 South LaGrande Ave.
          Princeton, MN 55371

22. The Source

The Source, a subsidiary of Reader's Digest, provides access to more than 1,200 programs and services in a variety of subject areas, including agriculture. It carries the Commodity News Service general news reports and daily price activities for major commodities. The system also supplies news and commentary on current business trends along with updated listings of stocks, bonds, commodities, and futures.

ADDRESS: The Source
          Source Telecomputing
          1616 Anderson Road
          McLean, VA 22102

23. Telplan

Telplan is a timesharing computer service with several interactive problem-solving packages. Its agricultural programs are in the areas of farm finance and animal nutrition, and it offers family finance and human nutrition programs as well. It is operated by Michigan State University and is available nationwide.

ADDRESS: Telplan—Michigan State University
Room 27 Agriculture Hall
Department of Agricultural Economics
Michigan State University
East Lansing, Ml 48824-1039

24. USDA Online

USDA Online delivers news and other current information from USDA's Office of Information. Services include the following reports as they are released: (1) USDA national news releases about policy and program announcements, (2) USDA regional and State news releases about program announcements, (3) outlook and situation report summaries, (4) Crop Reporting Board reports, report highlights, and summaries, (5) Foreign Agricultural Service reports and announcements on foreign crops, world production, and trade, (6) Economic Research Service report abstracts, (7) a daily agricultural news summary called "AG a.m.," and (8) a weekly "Farm Paper Letter" for farm magazine and newspaper editors and others interested in the summary and highlights of USDA reports for the week.

Through USDA Online, users can also access COIN (see p. 24-25) and several other data bases. Another communications network available to users of USDA Online is an electronic mail service linking various offices at USDA and the State Extension Services, land-grant Universities, State Departments of Agriculture, other Federal and State agencies, and other organizations interested in agriculture.

ADDRESS: News Division, Room 404-A
Office of Information
U.S. Department of Agriculture
Washington, D.C. 20250

Rural Telephone Lines

One question to consider when you are selecting a computer system to be used in a rural area is whether your telephone line is adequate for potential users in your area. You must have a private line. Line quality is also important; excessive line noise or dips and surges in power may cause the communications system to disconnect you.

In the future, farmers will be able to get information by satellite rather than through the phone, which could eventually be a cost saver for those who are far from the information source.

OTHER COMPUTER DEVELOPMENTS AT USDA

Besides online information services, there are several other computer developments available through USDA that are of use to farmers and ranchers. Many USDA agencies are using computers to disseminate information. Here is a partial list:

Since 1981, the Foreign Agricultural Service (FAS) has been releasing information electronically that previously had been distributed as publications through the mail.

The FAS electronic information system includes agricultural trade leads received from agricultural attaches relating to potential purchases of commodities by foreign buyers.

The Federal Crop Insurance Corporation (FCIC), in cooperation with the Extension Service, has developed two software packages to help farmers make decisions about the kind and amount of crop insurance they will need. ARCIE (All Risk Crop Insurance Evaluation) comes in "mini" and "complete" versions.

Mini-ARCIE takes individual farm data and calculates a projected cash flow under various yield conditions with and without crop insurance. It takes about 15 minutes to run.

Complete-ARCIE, which takes about an hour, analyzes risk and loss probabilities over an extended period. It prompts farmers to enter expected prices and yields, and to include historical data.

Both programs examine the insurance options available—both public and private—and show how these options compare and how they complement each other. Federal Crop Insurance is currently available on about 30 major crops nationwide.

These programs are designed to run on most microcomputer models. Your State Extension Service, State Vocational Education Office, or your local crop insurance agent may already have the programs.

For further information, including how to obtain a copy of the program, write to:

> The ARCIE Project
> Department of Agricultural Economics
> 107 Agricultural Building
> Texas A&M University
> College Station, TX 77840

The **Agricultural Stabilization and Conservation Service** (ASCS) is planning to put small computers into all its county offices starting in 1985. They will keep lists of farmers and their acreage allotments and bases, record set-aside histories, and record and maintain the other myriad facts necessary to make the USDA farm programs work. The system will keep farm records, addresses for mailings, election registers, and records of payments. Even checks to pay farmers will be produced by the decentralized county computer systems.

The computers will also be tied into State systems and a central computer for some recordkeeping functions, and can be used for electronic mail and other communications.

One function of the new system will be to mesh FAS trade opportunity leads into the ASCS data base. This will permit a farmer or local agribusiness person to go into the ASCS office and immediately learn about trade leads reported by agricultural attaches. This program will go into operation during the mid-1980's.

The **Economic Research Service** (ERS) releases its Outlook and Situation reports through AGNET. Summaries of these are available through USDA Online.

LEARNING MORE ABOUT COMPUTERS
ON THE FARM

The computer field is changing so fast that it is difficult to keep up with the changes. One way to keep current is to join a users group for your particular brand of computer, or an agricultural users group. Another way to get up-to-date information about new computer hardware and software products is to read a private newsletter. Some of these are:

AgriComp
1001 East Walnut, Suite 201
Columbia, MO 65201

Agricultural Computing
Doane-Western, Inc.
8900 Manchester Road
St. Louis, MO 63144

Agricultural Microcomputing
Ridgetown College of Agricultural Technology
Ridgetown, Ontario
CANADA NOP 2CO

Compu-Farm
Alberta Agricultural
Box 2000
Olds, Alberta
CANADA TOM 1PO

Computer Farming Newsletter
Lloyd Dinkins
P.O. Box 22642
Memphis, TN 38122

Farm Computer News
Successful Farming
1716 Locust Street
Des Moines, IA 50336

Friendly Farm Computer Newsletter
FBS Systems, Inc.
P.O. Box 201
Aledo, IL 61231

GLOSSARY OF COMPUTER TERMS

Listed below are some of the shorthand or jargon terms in the computer field. Understanding these terms will help you discuss hardware and software systems and their operation.

ADDRESS: A number specifying a particular location in the computer's memory.

BASIC (Beginner's All-purpose Symbolic Instruction Code): A relatively easy-to-use computer language that comes with most small and personal computer systems.

BAUD RATE: The speed at which information is exchanged over communications lines, generally expressed in characters per second. 300 baud is the most common rate. It is equivalent to 30 characters per second.

BINARY: A two-digit numbering system based on the digits 0 and 1. It is the basis for calculations on all computers, and the basis for storing and retrieving information, including alphabet characters.

BIT: The smallest unit of information the computer recognizes. A bit is represented by the presence or absence of an electronic pulse, 0 or 1.

BUG: A fault or error in a computer program.

BYTE: A byte is composed of several bits, and is used to represent one character—such as a letter, number, or punctuation mark. The older microcomputer systems used 8 bits per byte, but the newer ones are based on 16 or 32 bits per byte.

CHIP: A thin silicon wafer on which electronic components are deposited lithographically in the form of integrated circuits.

COBOL (Common Business-Oriented Language): A high-level programing language widely used in business applications.

COMPUTER NETWORK: Two or more computers that are connected so they can exchange information.

COMPUTER PROGRAM: A collection of instructions that together direct the computer to perform a particular function.

CP/M (Control Program for Microprocessors): A popular operating system for small computers.

CPU (Central Processing Unit): The part of the computer that controls and organizes the operations of the other parts of the computer and does the calculations.

CRT (Cathode Ray Tube): A video screen that can be used for viewing output.

DATA: The information, such as numbers or letters, that are put into the computer system.

DEBUG: To remove the errors in a computer program.

DIAGNOSTIC: A program for detecting and isolating a problem or mistake in the computer system; features that allow systems or equipment to self-test for flaws.

DISK: A revolving plate on which data and programs are stored. Also called DISKETTE.

DISK DRIVE: A part of the computer system that reads and writes material on the disk. It can be part of the main hardware or a peripheral attached to the system.

DOCUMENTATION: 1. The instruction manual for a program (software) or piece of hardware. 2. The process of describing a computer program so others using the program can see how it works.

DOWNTIME: Any time a computer is not available or not working because of a machine fault or failure. Downtime includes repair delay time, repair time, and machine-spoiled work time.

EDIT: To change or add data to an existing document or program.

FLOPPY DISK: A small, flexible storage device made of magnetic material. It looks like a soft phonograph record and is usually 5¼ inches or 8 inches in diameter.

FORTRAN (FORmula TRANslation): A computer language widely used to solve scientific and engineering problems, mainly for large commercial systems.

GARBAGE: Meaningless information.

HARD COPY: A printout on paper of information from the computer.

HARDWARE: All the physical parts of the computer system, including the computer itself, the input and output equipment and peripherals, and the physical disk or tape equipment. (The computer programs are software.)

INPUT: The data that are put into the computer, or the process of putting it in.

INSTRUCTION: A group of bits that designates a specific computer operation.

INTEGRATED CIRCUIT: An electronic circuit or combination of circuits contained on semiconductor material, or chip.

INTERACTIVE: A computer system that allows two-way

communication between the user and the computer.

INTERFACE: A piece of equipment used to connect two parts of a computer system that cannot interact directly with each other.

K (kilobyte): A measure of computer memory capacity. Each K of information is 1,024 bytes.

LOAD: To put data or programs into a computer.

MAGNETIC TAPE: A recording device used to store programs and data. It resembles audio tape used in tape recorders.

MEMORY: That part of the computer that stores information. Also, the external material, such as floppy disks, hard disks, or cassette tapes that store information.

MICROCOMPUTER: A small computer in which the CPU is an integrated circuit deposited on a silicon chip.

MICROPROCESSOR: A silicon chip that is the central, controlling part of the computer.

MINICOMPUTER: A computer that is usually larger, more powerful, and more expensive than a microcomputer, but is smaller than a mainframe in memory and functions.

MODEM (MODulator/ DEModulator): A device used to attach a computer or one of its devices to a communication line, often a telephone.

OPERATING SYSTEM: A special group of programs which controls the overall operation of a computer system. It mediates between the hardware and the particular software program.

OUTPUT: The information generated by a computer.

PERIPHERAL: A device, such as a CRT, disk drive, or printer, used for entering or storing data into, or retrieving it from, the computer system.

PRINTER: An output device to print the information from a computer.

PROGRAM: A set of coded instructions directing a computer to perform a particular function.

PROGRAMING LANGUAGE: A special language of words and rules that is used to write programs so the computer can understand them.

RAM (Random Access Memory): The portion of the computer's memory in which data, instructions, and other information are stored temporarily. Also called read-write memory.

ROM (Read Only Memory): The portion of the computer's memory that contains information and instructions that are stored permanently. This memory cannot be altered or added to.

SEMICONDUCTOR: A material such as silicon with a conductivity between that of a metal and an insulator. It is used in the manufacture of solid-state devices such as diodes, transistors, and the complex integrated circuits that comprise computer logic circuits.

SOFTWARE: A general term for computer programs, procedural rules, and sometimes the documentation involved in the operation of a computer.

SYSTEM: The computer and all its related components, including hardware and software, that work together.

TERMINAL: A peripheral device through which information is entered into or extracted from the computer, usually with a keyboard and an output device such as a CRT or printer.

TIMESHARING: A method by which more than one person can use a computer at the same time at separate terminals.

TURNKEY SYSTEM: A computer system that has all hardware and software installed. Supposedly, all you have to do is turn it on.

WORD PROCESSING: Typing, editing, storing, and printing text with a computer.

The mention of commercial products, services, or companies does not constitute endorsement by the U.S. Department of Agriculture. If additional computer services of interest to the agricultural community are available, we would be glad to consider them for inclusion in possible revisions of this bulletin.

Lector House believes that a society develops through a two-fold approach of continuous learning and adaptation, which is derived from the study of classic literary works spread across the historic timeline of literature records. Therefore, we aim at reviving, repairing and redeveloping all those inaccessible or damaged but historically as well as culturally important literature across subjects so that the future generations may have an opportunity to study and learn from past works to embark upon a journey of creating a better future.

This book is a result of an effort made by Lector House towards making a contribution to the preservation and repair of original ancient works which might hold historical significance to the approach of continuous learning across subjects.

HAPPY READING & LEARNING!

LECTOR HOUSE LLP
E-MAIL: lectorpublishing@gmail.com